Exploring an Ocean Tide Pool

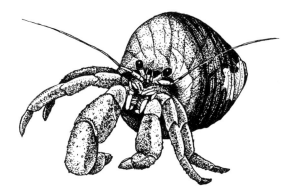

EXPLORING AN
Ocean Tide Pool

Jeanne Bendick
Illustrated by Todd Telander

A Redfeather Book

HENRY HOLT AND COMPANY · NEW YORK

The author wishes to thank Craig Strang, Director,
Ocean Studies Program, Lawrence Hall of Science,
University of California at Berkeley,
for his careful reading of the manuscript.

Photo credits: page viii (low tide scene with Pisaster sea stars), © Nancy Sefton;
page 10 (intertidal algae), Animals / Animals © Anne Wertheim; page 19
(hermit crab), Animals / Animals © Fred E. Unverhau; page 30 (purple sea
urchin test with live sea urchins), Animals / Animals © Doug Wechsler; page 38
(club-tipped anemones), © Brian Parker / Tom Stack and Associates; page 50
(Monterey Bay by full moon), Earth Scenes © Robert P. Comport.

First edition
Published by Henry Holt and Company, Inc.,
115 West 18th Street, New York, New York 10011.
Published simultaneously in Canada by Fitzhenry & Whiteside Ltd.,
91 Granton Drive, Richmond Hill, Ontario L4B 2N5.

Library of Congress Cataloging-in-Publication Data
Bendick, Jeanne.
    Exploring an ocean tide pool / Jeanne Bendick :
    illustrated by Todd Telander.
    (A Redfeather book)
    Includes index.
    Summary: Describes the plants and animals of an ocean tide pool
and their dependent interrelationships.
    ISBN 0-8050-2043-8
    1. Tide pool ecology—Juvenile literature. 2. Ocean—Juvenile
literature. [1. Tide pool ecology. 2. Ecology.] I. Telander,
Todd, ill. II. Title. III. Series.
QH541.5.S35B46   1992
574.5'2636—dc20   91-34572

Printed in the United States of America
on acid-free paper. ∞

10 9 8 7 6 5 4 3 2 1

To Son, Bob,
who protects tide pools
                        —J. B.

To Deborah,
with thanks for her
support and enthusiasm
                        —T. T.

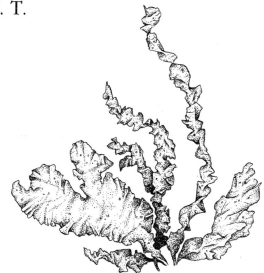

Contents

1 · *The Tide Pool*   1

2 · *What's Growing in the Tide Pool?*   9

3 · *At Home in the Tide Pool*   17

4 · *Who Eats Whom and How*   31

5 · *More About Who Eats Whom*   39

6 · *The Big Ocean*   51

Index   55

one

The Tide Pool

All over the earth, wherever there are oceans, there are seashores, where the sea and the land come together. The wind blows, the waves splash and crash, the beach bugs hop, and the shorebirds fly.

When the tide is high, the seashore is almost completely covered with water. Then, when the tide goes out, the water moves down the shore again, out to sea. The water in all the oceans rises and falls that way on seashores all over the earth. On most of them, twice a day the tide is high and twice a day it's low.

The part of the seashore that the tides cover and uncover is called the intertidal zone. For part of the time the intertidal zone is underwater. For part of the time it is out of the water.

Pisaster sea stars at low tide

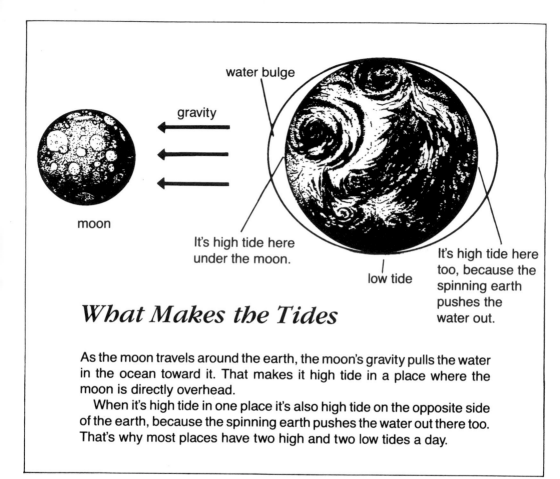

gravity

water bulge

moon

It's high tide here under the moon.

low tide

It's high tide here too, because the spinning earth pushes the water out.

What Makes the Tides

As the moon travels around the earth, the moon's gravity pulls the water in the ocean toward it. That makes it high tide in a place where the moon is directly overhead.

When it's high tide in one place it's also high tide on the opposite side of the earth, because the spinning earth pushes the water out there too. That's why most places have two high and two low tides a day.

The intertidal zone does not look the same everywhere. It may be grassy and muddy, sandy, or rocky.

When the tide is low on a rocky shore, most of the rocks are out of the water. But there are pools in and between the rocks that trap the ocean water even at low tide. The pools are called tide pools. Most of them aren't even big enough to swim in. They look like rocky bathtubs full of plants, animals, and ocean water.

Walking along a rocky shore, you could go right by a tide pool and never notice it. But you'd miss a lot.

Stop and watch for a minute or two, and you will begin to see things move. Get down close and keep looking. You will find yourself watching a busy, crowded neighborhood. Animals live everywhere in the tide pool.

A rocky little pool of water on a beach may seem a strange place for so many animals to live, but it's not. All over the earth, on land and in water, wherever plants and animals can live, they do. They live together and share the space as neighbors.

Everywhere, each small neighborhood is a part of a bigger neighborhood, which is a part of a bigger one, right up to the biggest—the earth.

A tide pool is a small neighborhood. It's a part of the bigger neighborhood of the intertidal zone. The intertidal zone stretches around the earth, wherever the land and the ocean meet.

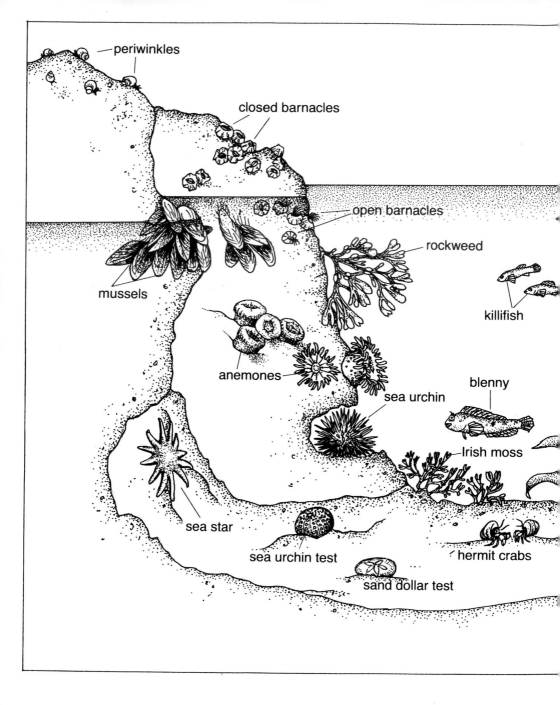

periwinkles

closed barnacles

open barnacles

rockweed

killifish

mussels

anemones

sea urchin

blenny

Irish moss

sea star

sea urchin test

hermit crabs

sand dollar test

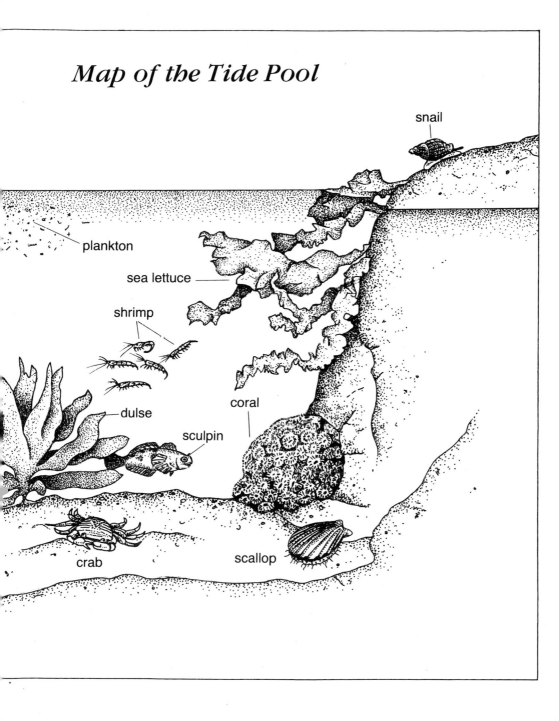

Map of the Tide Pool

snail

plankton

sea lettuce

shrimp

dulse

sculpin

coral

crab

scallop

Most of the earth is covered by ocean. The ocean is so big that no one person can ever see all the kinds of things that live in it. But you can find out a lot about life in the ocean by exploring life in a very small ocean—one tide pool.

When you are exploring the pool, you may not see some of the animal neighbors at first. You may not even think of them as animals.

Some of the animals in the tide pool look like stones. Some look like plants. Some are hidden. Some move so slowly that you can't believe they are moving. Some move so fast that you're not sure you even saw them.

The biggest animals in the pool are smaller than your hand. The smallest ones are so small that you'll never see them without a microscope.

The neighbors in the tide pool look very different from one another. But they don't just happen to be the size, shape, or color they are. They don't just happen to do the things you'll see them do.

Like animals everywhere, everything about them is specially adapted for the life they live and the place they live in.

You'll have a good time getting to know the tide

pool inhabitants, so stay and watch. Wear your sneakers and old jeans or a bathing suit. You'll probably get wet. Bring your lunch. It will take a while. Bring a magnifying glass. You'll see more.

You'll have to adjust your eyes for looking small. You are a giant from another place, watching a small world to find out what life is like there. If you could make yourself small enough to spend a day in the tide pool, you would see some wonderful things.

Now is a good time. The tide is low. The water in the tide pool is quiet.

Some of the neighbors are under the water. Some of them are out of the water. Herds of snails called rough periwinkles are grazing on the rocks. The snails are eating plants, which they scrape off the rocks with their rough, zipperlike tongues. They scrape so hard that where there are lots of snails, the rock gets worn down.

Stuck on the rocks in thick patches are thousands of other animals. At first these look like patches of sharp, white stones. But when you look again, you see that they are small shells, closed up tight. Inside are animals called barnacles.

Close to the barnacles are the snail relatives with the shells that look like striped pointy hats. They are limpets.

Below the barnacles and limpets are crowds of bigger, dark blue shells. Inside are animals called mussels. Their shells are closed up tight too.

Are you looking small? Or imagining yourself small? Then with your new, small self start down into the tide pool.

Go down past those rubbery-looking bumps on the rocks. The bumps are not rocks. They don't look like plants. They don't look like animals, but they are. They are anemones.

Near them on the rocks a sea star is hanging on with the hundreds of feet underneath its five spiny arms. The sea star isn't moving.

Watch it! There's a creature that looks something like a pincushion full of fat pins! It's an animal called a sea urchin.

Now you're on the bottom. All around you, under your feet and over your head, is a jungle of tide pool plants.

two

What's Growing in the Tide Pool?

*T*he plants growing in the tide pool almost all belong to the same plant group. They are all algae. People usually call them seaweeds.

Like plants everywhere, the tide pool plants are working. They are making food. All green plants can make their own food from sunlight.

Some algae look bright green. Some don't look green at all. They look orange, pink, red, purple, or almost white. Some look brown or yellow. The orange, pink, red, and purple patches on the rocks are also algae. So are those slippery black smears up on the dry rocks. But in every plant, the green is there and working.

While they are making food, plants give off the oxygen that animals need to stay alive. Animals can't turn sunlight into food or make their own

9

oxygen, so animals on land and in the water depend on plants for those things.

On land, usually it's easy to tell what's a plant and what's an animal. Most plants stay in one place. Most animals move around. But in the tide pool, things are different. Many plants move around. Some animals seem to be rooted in place. Don't be too sure you'll be able to tell a plant from an animal when you see one.

Algae don't look like land plants. Some look like smears of color on a rock. Some look like ribbons and some like shoelaces. Others look like rugs, lace, or feathers. Some are as thin and light as spiderwebs. Some are hollow. Some have knots, and some have little gas-filled balloons in them.

The tide pool plants don't feel like land plants, either. The ones on the bottom of the pool are like a thick, bouncy rug. The short, bright-colored ones growing on rocks and on shells feel like velvet. And when you touch the bigger ones that are attached to the rocks and floating in the tide pool, they feel slippery and rubbery.

Light, thin, hollow, or full of gas balloons, seaweeds float, bend, and sway. Unless they are very

Intertidal algae

Photosynthesis

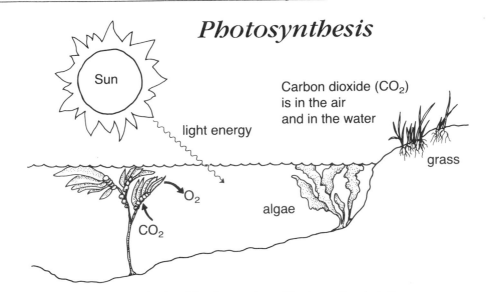

Most plants can make food for themselves. Photosynthesis is the name given to the process. (*Photo* means "light" and *synthesis* means "to put together.")

All plants contain a green pigment called chlorophyll. Chlorophyll captures light energy from the sun. A plant puts the light energy together with water and a common gas called carbon dioxide to make the carbohydrates, or sugars, they use for food. While they make food, plants give off oxygen into the air. Plants in the ocean produce nearly half the oxygen on the earth. They are very important to the health of the planet.

Seaweed may look brown or purple or red, but the chlorophyll is there under the other colors. Even tiny, one-celled algae have chlorophyll.

Land plants make food only in their leaves, but seaweeds make food throughout the plant.

short, they move with the water. If the water is rough, pieces may break off.

Water slides and drips off the slippery seaweeds. Even at low tide, when a lot of the seaweeds are out of the water, the drip, drip, drip keeps everything underneath them wet. Many of the tide pool animals are under seaweeds at low tide.

Most of the seaweeds in the tide pool are the kind called rockweeds. When you take a close look, you see that they are growing right on the rocks. They are hanging on with special kinds of grabbers and holders called holdfasts. Some holdfasts look like fingers. Some look like flat sink stoppers. Holdfasts look something like roots, but they aren't roots.

The roots of land plants go down into the soil and soak up minerals and water. Then that liquid moves up from the roots, through the stem and into the leaves, where the plant makes its food.

Algae take in water and minerals all over, and they make their food in every part of themselves. So algae don't have roots, stems, and leaves. They don't have flowers, either.

The plants around you are food for some of the tide pool animals. The plants also give them homes and hiding places.

The seaweed is like a jungle full of animals.

Underwater Plants

The 20,000 species of underwater plants are all called algae. There are four main groups of algae:

1. Blue-green algae are so tiny that one of them is invisible to the eye, but many of them together make rock surfaces dark or slimy.
2. Red algae, like dulse and Irish moss, don't all look red. Some look purple. Some look orange.
3. Brown algae, like rockweed and winged kelp, grow on rocky shores and in shallow water. They are used for food and to make gelatin, vitamins, and fertilizer.
4. Green algae, like sea lettuce and *Enteromorpha,* are the most common seaweeds. They were probably the ancestors of all land plants. Most green algae live in shallow water.

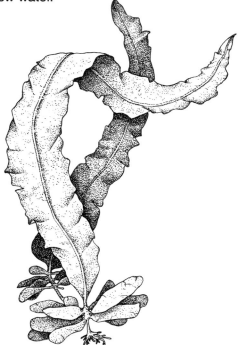

An extract of Irish moss called carrageenan is used to make ice cream, face cream, paint, and many other foods and cosmetics.

Dulse has bright, purple-red branches. In many places people eat it as a vegetable.

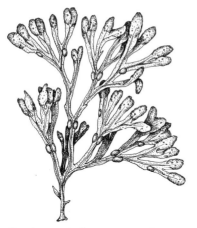

Rockweed also grows all over rocky shores. The little air bladders along the stems keep it floating.

Winged kelp grows where the water is cold.

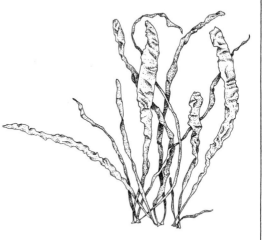

Sea lettuce grows all along rocky seashores in the intertidal zone.

Enteromorpha looks like grass. Its blades are hollow.

There are more animals than you can count. Little fish that were left when the tide went out are there. So are tiny shrimp. You can see right through them! There are baby crabs, as small as a dime and smaller. There are baby sea stars and tiny sea worms. Snails hang and crawl on the seaweed. If you peek into splits and holes in the seaweed, you'll see baby snails.

Look close and you will see some things that are even smaller. There are eggs on the seaweed and under it—eggs in cases, eggs in bubbles, eggs just floating. Most of those eggs will hatch, but only a few of the new animals will grow up. Most will be eaten by other animals.

That's the way it's supposed to be. If all the eggs hatched and grew up, the ocean would be solid with animals.

Water bugs swim and hop in and out of the seaweed, but everything down there isn't small. Sea urchins live there. So do big crabs.

A crab pops out and looks at you. Its eyes are on little rods up on top of its head. It wiggles them, then ducks into a crevice. For many, but not all, of the tide pool neighbors, the seaweed is home.

three

At Home in the Tide Pool

*T*he tide pool is one of the most crowded neighborhoods on the earth. For its size, it is more crowded than the biggest city. Maybe a million animals live there—maybe more than a million.

Animals live on the plants, under them, and in them.

Animals live in the sand and among the ground-up shells at the bottom.

Animals live on the rocks and under the rocks. Down here in the tide pool, there are animals everywhere.

Some of the animals are small fish. They come in with the tide. Sometimes they go out on the next tide. Sometimes they stay for a while. There isn't enough food or water for bigger fish to make their homes in the tide pool neighborhood.

17

Many of the animals have shells as houses. Some, like the snails, have a single shell. Some, like the mussels, have two shells hinged together. Some animals live in the shells that other animals have left. Some of the animals with shell houses hang on to the rocks. Some hang on to the shells of other animals.

Being able to hang on is one important thing that helps animals and plants survive in the tide pool. Where the ocean comes and goes and the waves crash, the water can be rough. If they can't hang on, animals and plants can be tumbled around or washed away.

Nothing in the world can hang on better than a barnacle.

When barnacles are very young and very small, they swim free. One day they settle on a rock or other hard surface, cement themselves in place, make shells, and that's that. The cement they make is so strong that even after a barnacle dies, its shell hangs on to the rock. You can see these empty shells, like little cups crowded in among the live barnacles.

Hermit crab

Are they really empty? Look inside.

They may be empty of barnacles, but some hold baby snails, no bigger than specks. Some hold even tinier eggs.

Now, at low tide, all the live barnacles are closed up tight. Many of the tide pool animals can live out of the water for part of the day. But most of them can't get the oxygen they need from the air, as land animals do. Sea plants make oxygen in the water, and the tide pool animals get the oxygen they need from the water. So they must have ways of keeping wet, even when the tide is out.

If you are around when the tide starts to go out, you can hear the barnacles clicking shut, while they are still full of water. Each barnacle keeps enough seawater inside its shell to keep its gills wet until the tide comes in again.

That limpet over there—the snail relative with the shell that looks like a pointy hat—has another way of hanging on and of keeping the water in.

Like all snails, a limpet has one big foot with a strong suction cup on it. Before the tide goes out, while there is still water in its shell, the limpet

Breathing Underwater

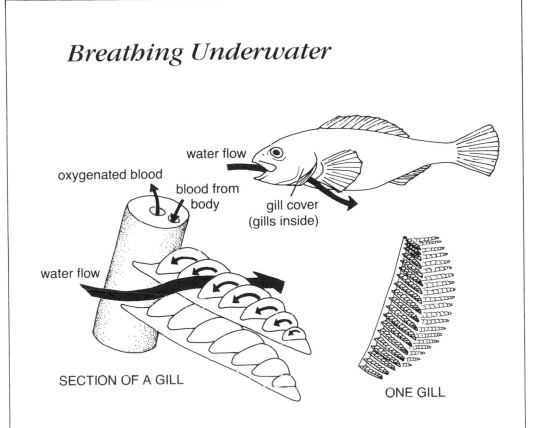

water flow

oxygenated blood

blood from body

gill cover (gills inside)

water flow

SECTION OF A GILL

ONE GILL

All animals need oxygen to live. Land animals take oxygen out of the air through their lungs, which pass the oxygen into the bloodstream. Water contains oxygen too. Most sea creatures have to extract the oxygen they need from water.

Fish have gills to help them do this. A fish constantly takes in water through its mouth and pumps it over its gills. As the water passes the gills, blood vessels there absorb oxygen out of the water. Then the water is pushed out through the back of the gill cover.

Most marine animals have gills. Other sea creatures absorb oxygen directly into their bloodstreams.

Fish

Fish are the only tide pool animals with backbones. Backboned animals are called vertebrates.

Many fish can change color quickly to camouflage themselves. Tide pool fish are especially good at camouflage.

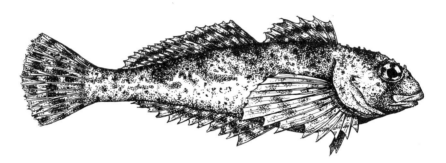

Sculpins lie on the bottom of the tide pool, hiding in seaweed. Their colors match the seaweed's exactly. The fins of a sculpin are big and spiny. They can be extended up and sideways to look threatening, or down to hang on to the bottom of the tide pool.

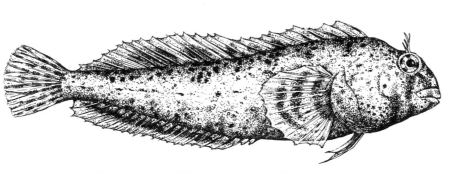

Blennies are tide pool fish too. They prop
themselves up on their bottom fins to observe
their surroundings and even to walk, the way
killies do. Sometimes blennies sunbathe on
rocks.

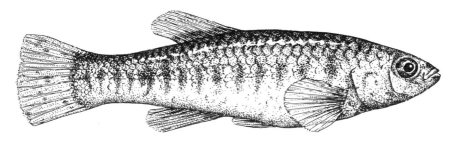

Killifish, also called killies, live almost
everywhere that's seaweedy, along the coasts of
North and South America, Asia, and Africa.
These fish aren't particular—they can even live
in freshwater ponds. Killies come in with the tide.
If the sides of the tide pool are shallow, they can
use their fins almost like legs to climb out and
crawl to another pool or pond if it's not too far.

Hermit Crabs

A hermit crab has no shell to protect it. It has big, sharp claws and a hard covering called an exoskeleton on its front, but the rest of its body is soft and unprotected. So the hermit crab lives in empty snail shells.

As the hermit crab grows, it has to move into bigger and bigger shells. This crab's old shell is getting too small, so it's looking for a bigger one on the tide pool floor.

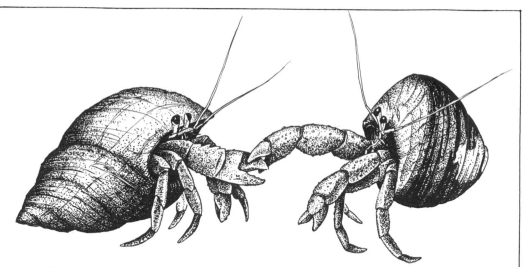

That one? The hermit rolls it over and looks at it. Too small. That one? It has another hermit crab in it! Sometimes hermit crabs fight each other for a shell. These two have a short claw-pulling match, then the house-hunting hermit moves on.

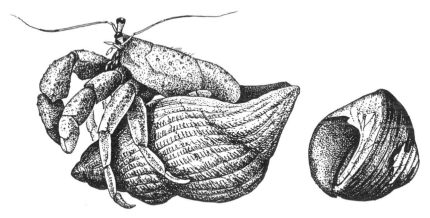

That one? Just right. And it's empty. The hermit crab takes a quick look around to be sure there are no enemies ready to grab it when it is unprotected. Then it jumps out of the old shell, backs into the new one, and uses its biggest claw to close the shell opening up tight.

Mollusks

Mollusks are a group of creatures with soft bodies usually protected by shells. Some, like the snails, have a single shell. They have a head with tentacles and one foot for walking and digging. A snail can pull in its foot and close up tight with a hard disk called an operculum. The bivalve mollusks—clams, oysters, mussels, and scallops—have two hard shells, joined by a hinge. (*Bivalve* means "two shells.") A muscle works the hinge to open and close the shells. Clams have double siphons. One siphon sucks in food, water, and oxygen; the other gets rid of wastes.

A mussel spins strong threads from its foot. The threads glue it to rocks or other mussels.

A scallop can jet-propel itself in any direction by snapping its shells open and shut.

Snails are scavengers and grazers.
The sharp teeth on their tongues
shred food. Some snails also drill
through the shells of other mollusks.

A clam opens its shell
to take in food and water.

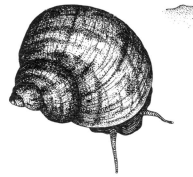

A rough periwinkle spends
so much time out of water
that its gills can take oxygen
from the air.

Whelks are bigger, fancier snails
than periwinkles. Whelks lay their
eggs in egg cases that look like
strings of small potato chips.
A string of egg cases may
be a yard long.

presses so hard against the rock that the water stays inside its shell and keeps the limpet wet until the tide comes in again.

Some people think that limpets, like barnacles, always stay in the same place, but they don't. Like other snails, limpets move around to graze on algae. Then each limpet comes back to one special place on the rock. Its shell fits exactly against the rock in that place. Nobody knows just how the limpet gets its shell to fit so closely or how it always finds its way back to its own place.

The mussels have their own way of hanging on. They live fastened to the rocks and to one another with strong threads that they spin themselves.

Sometimes those threads break. Then you might see a mussel at work, gluing itself on again.

Out of one side of the mussel's double shell comes its foot. Out of its foot comes a new thread. If you get close enough, you can see some sticky stuff forming at the end of that thread.

The thread floats to the rock and catches. Out comes another thread. It floats to the nearest mussel and catches. Soon the mussel is glued down again.

No matter how thick the crowds of mussels and barnacles are on the rocks, there is still room for other animals to live among them. Snails do. So do bugs and thousands of worms. Young barnacles have glued themselves onto some of the mussel shells. Plants grow on the mussel shells too.

Down on the bottom of the tide pool are more animals, in one shell or two.

There are clam shells that washed in with the last high tide. Some scallop shells got into the tide pool by mistake too. They look fancy, pink and green. Animals and plants are growing on the scallops.

Here comes a snail across the bottom. It's moving fast, for a snail. And look at those claws. Look at those eight legs. Look at those eyes, up on stalks. It isn't a snail at all—it's a crab in a snail shell! It's a hermit crab that is getting too big for its shell.

All the while you've been wandering through the tide pool, the tide has been coming in—dripping, sloshing, and washing into the tide pool. And now the action really begins. Because when the tide comes in, it's eating time in the neighborhood.

four

Who Eats Whom and How

*T*he mud snails don't wait for the tide. They are almost always walking around the rocks at the sides of the tide pool and on the bottom. They are part of the neighborhood garbage squad. They eat any dead stuff that's around. Animals like that are called scavengers. Scavengers keep things cleaned up in big and little neighborhoods all over the earth.

The mud snails are walking? How? On feet, of course.

On land, most animals have several feet—two, four, six, eight, or more. Some of the tide pool animals also have several feet, but the most useful number of feet down here seems to be one.

All the snails have one foot. They don't hop on

Purple sea urchin test with live sea urchins

it. They move themselves along by pushing that foot out in front of them and then pulling themselves up to where the foot is.

If you pick up a snail, it will pull in its foot. Then it slams shut the door to its shell with a sort of horny button called an operculum, which fits exactly into the shell opening.

A clam also has one foot. It walks by pulling itself along on its foot. It uses its foot for digging, too. If there is enough sand or mud, a clam can dig itself out of sight in no time. That's how a clam gets away from clam eaters, if it can.

Here comes a clam eater now. The sea star has climbed down from a rock and is moving toward the clam.

The sea star climbs on top and wraps its arms around the clam. This clam has a shell that is easy to open, but if a clam is closed up tight in a hard, thick shell, a tug-of-war starts. The sea star tries to pull the clam's two shells open. The clam uses the strong muscle between its shells to hold them shut.

If the sea star is big and the clam is small, the tug-of-war doesn't last very long. If they are almost the same size, it may go on for hours. But almost always, the sea star wins.

The sea star's mouth is underneath its body, where all its arms come together. Even if the sea star can only get the shell open a little bit, it can eat the clam. The sea star pushes its stomach out through its mouth and into the clamshell, where it surrounds the clam and digests it right there in the clam's shell.

Gently pick up the sea star and turn it over. It won't hurt you. Now you can see how it got the clamshell open and how it hangs on to the rocks. Under its arms are rows of tiny tubes with suction cups on the ends. The sea star clamps those suction cups on the top and bottom of the clam and pulls the shells apart.

Sea stars eat mussels, snails, and oysters too. Most of the other tide pool neighbors eat very tiny sea stars. No tide pool animal can eat a grown-up sea star, but some nearby neighbors do. Birds eat them. Out in the ocean very big snails eat them.

The snails munching on the rockweeds and the

Echinoderms

Echinoderms are a group of creatures that live only in the sea. They don't live on land or in fresh water. Echinoderms have spiny skins and hundreds of hollow, tube feet with suction cups on the bottom.

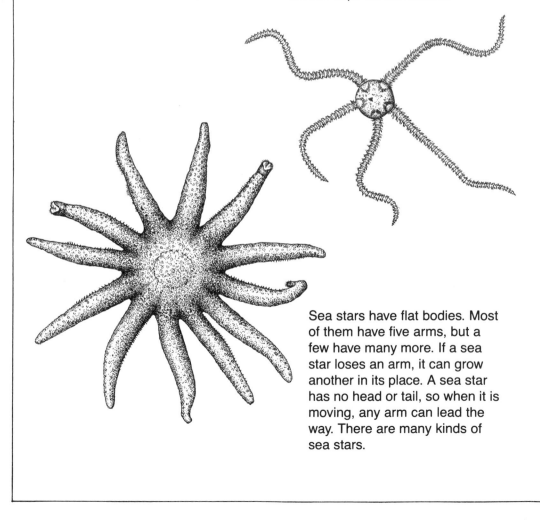

Sea stars have flat bodies. Most of them have five arms, but a few have many more. If a sea star loses an arm, it can grow another in its place. A sea star has no head or tail, so when it is moving, any arm can lead the way. There are many kinds of sea stars.

Sea urchins look like spiny balls.
Their round shells, called tests,
protect their soft bodies. The
tests have bumps and holes.
When sea urchins are alive,
spines are mounted on the
bumps and their tube feet
come in and out of the holes.

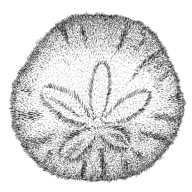

Sand dollars are a lot like sea urchins, but their bodies are
flatter. Sand dollar shells have beautiful patterns on each side.

snails grazing on the rocks are plant eaters, but many other kinds of snails are meat eaters. Over there is a snail sitting on a mussel. You can't really see what's happening, but the snail is sitting down to dinner. It's using its long, sharp tongue to drill a neat little hole right through the mussel's shell. When the snail gets its tongue through, it will eat the mussel.

The meat-eating snails eat mussels and clams, oysters and barnacles. They can wipe out those animals in a tide pool if something else doesn't eat the snails. Usually, something does. Crabs eat them. Sea stars eat them. So do birds.

Now, under the water, all over the rocks, the barnacles are opening and closing their shells. When the shells open, little feathers come out. It looks as if all the barnacles are waving.

What looks like feathers are actually the barnacles' legs. They are sweeping something into their shells with their feathery feet.

The tide is bringing thousands and millions of tiny somethings into the pool. You can't see each one. But if you look hard, maybe you can see them all together, like a mist in the water.

A fresh supply of the most common kind of living things in the world comes in with the tide. They are called plankton. Their name comes from a word that means "wanderer" or "drifter."

five

More About Who Eats Whom

One way or another, plankton are food for all the animals in the sea. Many animals eat plankton. Others eat the animals that eat plankton.

Some plankton are tiny, one-celled animals that will never get any bigger. Some plankton are tiny sea babies that will grow into many kinds of sea animals if they aren't eaten first. They will grow into fish, shrimp, or crabs, clams, sea stars, or barnacles.

Most of the plankton are plants. Billions and billions of them float near the top of the ocean, where they can get energy from the sun. Each one uses that energy to make food for itself. Each one gives off oxygen while it is making food.

Club-tipped anemones

Even if they were big enough to see, you wouldn't recognize plankton as plants. There are thousands of kinds, and their shapes are beautiful.

Watch the sea urchin. Its spines are beginning to move, this way, that way. When plankton drift by, the sea urchin sticks out its feet and catches them. The sea urchin will eat almost anything that is drifting around.

The sea urchin has many tube feet, and each foot has a suction cup on the end. Mostly the sea urchin sits, but it can move fast, walking on its spines, its feet, and even on its five sharp teeth. The sea urchin's mouth is underneath its body, like the mouth of its relative, the sea star. Its sharp teeth can grind up plankton, little snails, barnacles, and sometimes mussels.

Do clams eat plankton? Watch. The clam opens its shells, and two tubes come out of one side. These are the clam's siphons. The clam pulls water and plankton in through one, and spits out water and anything it doesn't want through the other.

Mussels eat plankton too. They open their shells, take in water and plankton, and strain out the plankton. Then they sweep the water back out.

Plankton

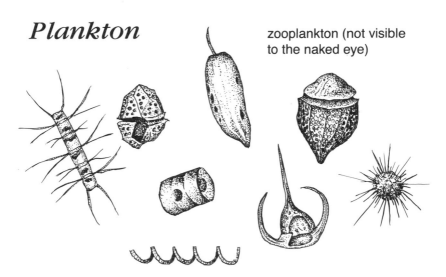

zooplankton (not visible to the naked eye)

Some plankton are plants, called phytoplankton. Some are animals, called zooplankton. Some are the larvae (young) of other sea creatures like barnacles and oysters. Some are plankton their whole lives. Most are tiny, but others are huge. Even if the plankton are single cells, each one must do for itself all the things a complex plant or animal does.

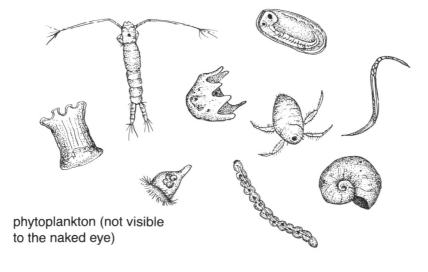

phytoplankton (not visible to the naked eye)

Cnidaria

Jellyfish and anemones belong to a group called cnidaria (they used to be called coelenterates). Cnidarians have hollow guts. Cnidarians have jellylike bodies called polyps, which are closed at one end and open at the other. The open end, which is the mouth, is surrounded by tentacles armed with tiny stinging cells. The tentacles catch any food that is drifting by, paralyze it with poison, and then push it into the mouth. Cnidarians also defend themselves with their tentacles.

This is a Portuguese man-of-war jellyfish. On the beach it looks like a deflated purple balloon. Don't touch it! It's very poisonous.

Jellyfish are almost all water. They are shaped like umbrellas, with tentacles around the edges. The mouth is under the umbrella. Jellyfish drift through the water, opening and closing their umbrellas to pump water and food into their mouths.

Anemones can move slowly, but usually they don't move at all. They fasten onto rocks or shells, or even onto the backs of crabs. When the tide is out, anemones usually pull in their tentacles and close up so they don't dry out.

Corals are cnidaria too. Corals use the calcium in seawater to build solid structures around themselves. A coral animal's mouth is surrounded by tentacles that sweep food into the polyp. Most corals live in colonies. In tropical waters they build huge reefs.

open anemone

Cnidaria

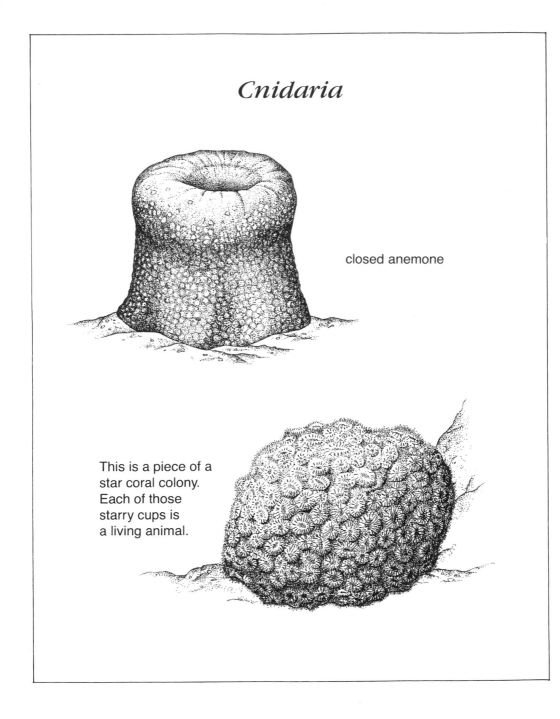

closed anemone

This is a piece of a
star coral colony.
Each of those
starry cups is
a living animal.

Everything comes and goes through the mussel's frilly, purple mantle.

The scallop that got in the tide pool by mistake eats in just about the same way, but there is something special about its mantle. Can you see those bright blue dots on it, just inside the scallop's shells? Those are the scallop's very good eyes, more than thirty of them!

A scallop can move fast, up off the bottom and through the water. It opens its shells and claps them shut, shooting out a jet of water. In the ocean, scallops move a few feet with every clap.

Other tiny young sea animals are coming in with the tide. They are bigger plankton—about the size of tiny dots. They look like sparkles in the water. They eat the smaller plankton too. Bigger meat eaters eat them.

Remember those anemones on the rocks? Look at them now. They don't look anything like the bumps you saw earlier. Even though they are not flowers or plants at all, they have opened up into what looks like a whole garden of flowers. Some have pink petals, some have white, and some are fluffy tan or gray. Many are green.

Crustaceans

The crabs in the tide pool belong to the group crustaceans. Crustaceans usually have ten jointed legs, two pairs of antennas, and an exoskeleton that surrounds and protects the body.

Some crustaceans, like crabs, also have a single, hard carapace on their backs. Most crustaceans are meat eaters. The larger ones, like crabs and lobsters, are scavengers too.

Barnacles are crustaceans that live inside the volcano-shaped shells they fasten to rocks, wood, or bigger shells. Some barnacles even live on whales.

The tide pool barnacles open their shells when the tide comes in, and their feathery, jointed legs pull floating food into their mouths. When the tide goes out, barnacles close up tight, trapping a little seawater inside their shells.

Crabs use their big front claws for fighting, for defense, for seizing food, for walking, and for digging.

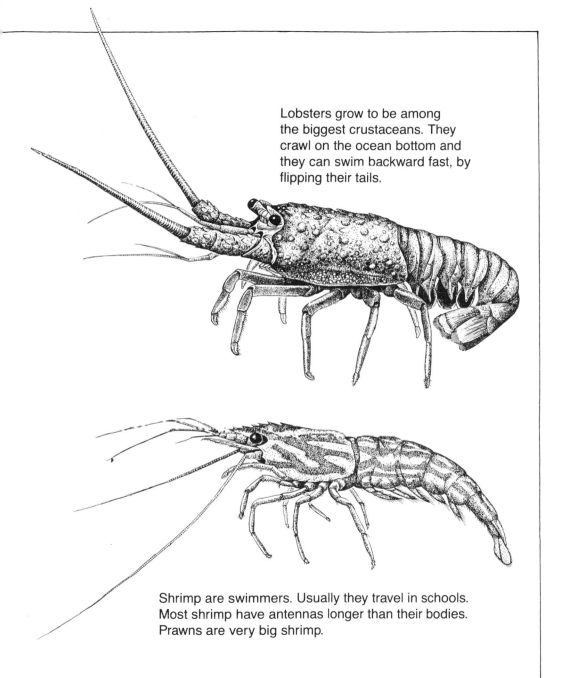

Lobsters grow to be among the biggest crustaceans. They crawl on the ocean bottom and they can swim backward fast, by flipping their tails.

Shrimp are swimmers. Usually they travel in schools. Most shrimp have antennas longer than their bodies. Prawns are very big shrimp.

Anemones are meat-eating animals, and they eat almost anything they can grab. When something drifts by an anemone, the things that look like flower petals grab it, close around it, and pull it into the anemone's mouth.

The anemones look as if they are stuck in one place, but they aren't. Like so many of their neighbors, anemones have one big foot with a suction cup on it. Once in a while an anemone will move a little way on its foot, then settle down again.

There are about a thousand kinds of anemones in the ocean. Some are big enough to eat a big fish. Some are small enough to live fastened onto the shells of other animals.

Hermit crabs and anemones often live together that way. When one eats, the other gets the leftovers that float away. When a hermit crab changes shells, sometimes it uses its claws to move its anemone to the new shell.

The tide tumbles a clam with a broken shell into the tide pool, and out come the crabs—from under the seaweed, from under the rocks, from holes they have dug. There are all kinds of crabs—blue, red, and green, spotted and speckled, all sizes.

They grab at the clam meat with their claws, pulling it apart and fighting one another for it. If a crab gets hurt, the others will eat it too.

For a crab, that's how life is. Crabs eat whatever is around. They help keep the pool clean that way.

Now the worms are out. There are many kinds of worms. Some are as big as new pencils. Some are as small as hairs.

The worms are hunters. They are also hunted. Worms eat worms and other tiny animals. Crabs, shrimp, and the baby snails down in the seaweed eat little worms.

Here come the shrimp! There are big ones, chased in from the ocean by hungry fish, and little ones, up from the seaweed jungle. The big shrimp eat worms and very small fish. Bigger fish eat the shrimp.

Now, at high tide, the ocean tide pool isn't a small world by itself anymore. It is part of the big ocean.

A plastic bottle floats in. There is a sudden rainbow of colors on the surface of the pool. That's oil pollution. What is in the ocean becomes part of the tide pool.

Monterey Bay by full moon

six

The Big Ocean

You can tell a lot about what's happening in the big ocean by what's happening in the tide pools.

In the little ocean pool you have been exploring, the water is usually clean and clear. There are many kinds of healthy plants. And there are many different kinds of animals, each living its own kind of life in its own way.

But not all tide pools look like yours. Some look unhealthy.

They may have junk in them—cans, plastic, bits of paper. The sand and pebbles on the bottom look scummy. The water is dirty. There might be oil or suds or chemicals in it.

Everything may be coated with slimy stuff. It's on the snails, the clams, and the mussels. Many of the barnacles are dead. This kind of tide pool isn't a good place for plants and animals to live.

A polluted tide pool doesn't look much like a garden. There are rockweed and a green alga called sea lettuce. The seaweeds look dirty. They don't smell clean and salty. They smell bad. Other kinds of algae aren't growing.

The living things in a tide pool depend on one another in so many ways that when pollution kills some, others can't stay alive. This doesn't happen only in tide pools. It happens in the ocean, too.

No matter where you live, at the seashore or thousands of miles away, you depend on the ocean for some very important things. So does every other living thing.

All animals need oxygen to stay alive. Plants make that oxygen. Most of it is made by billions and billions of tiny plankton drifting in the ocean—the phytoplankton.

All living things need water to stay alive. On land, most of that water comes from rain. But rain isn't "new" water that comes out of the sky. Rain begins as ocean water.

Heat from the sun pulls water vapor out of the ocean into the air. (The salt stays in the ocean.) Wind blows the water vapor around the earth. The

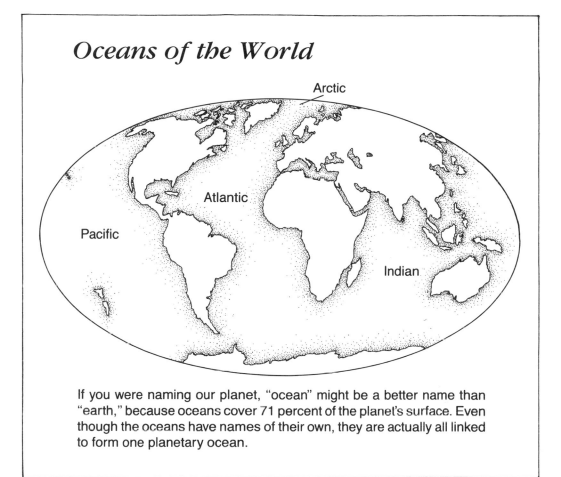

Oceans of the World

If you were naming our planet, "ocean" might be a better name than "earth," because oceans cover 71 percent of the planet's surface. Even though the oceans have names of their own, they are actually all linked to form one planetary ocean.

droplets of water come together into clouds. When the clouds get heavy, the water falls to the earth as rain. Finally, the water flows back into the ocean—not just clean rainwater, but also water with sewage, chemicals, oil, suds, fertilizer, and poisons.

So far, the big ocean has always been able to clean up the junk that comes into it from people. But more and more junk is coming into the ocean faster and faster. Maybe someday, if too much comes in, the big ocean won't be able to clean it all up. If it gets too dirty, the living things in the ocean can't stay alive.

Everywhere on the earth, people and other animals depend on the ocean for the air they breathe; for fresh, clean water; and for food. So keeping the ocean clean is important to everybody, not just to the mussels and barnacles, the snails and crabs, the shrimp and anemones, and all the other animals in the littlest ocean.

And now it's time to leave the tide pool.

Climb up through the seaweed, out of the water onto the rocks.

It may be slippery, so walk carefully up higher on the rocks, to where the tide doesn't come. When you look back, you can't even see where the tide pool is. It's all underwater. You can hardly believe that you were in it.

But the tide pool is still there. Maybe you can come back when the tide goes out again.

Index

Boldface indicates picture.

algae (seaweeds), **4–5,** 9–16, **14–15,** 28, 52
    animals living in, 13–16
    as food, 7, 28, 35–36
    photosynthesis by, 9, **12**
anemones, **4–5,** 8, **42–44,** 48

barnacles, **4–5,** 7, 18–20, 36, **46–47**
bivalves, **26–27**
blennies, 4–5, **22–23**
breathing, 20, **21, 26–27**

camouflage, **22–23**
carrageenan, **14–15**
chlorophyll, **12**
clams, **4–5, 26–27,** 29, 32–33, 36, 40, 48
cnidaria (coelenterates), **42–44**
    See also anemones, coral, jellyfish
coral, **4–5, 42**
crabs, **4–5,** 16, **46–47,** 48–49
    See also hermit crabs

crustaceans, **46–47**
    See also barnacles, crabs, lobsters, prawns, shrimp

dulse, **4–5, 14–15**

echinoderms, **34–35**
    See also sand dollars, sea stars, sea urchins
eggs, 16, 20
Enteromorpha, **14–15**

fish, 16, 17, **22–23**

gills, **21, 26–27**
grazing, 7, **26–27,** 28, 35–36

hermit crabs, **4–5, 24–25,** 29, 48
holdfasts, 13
hunting, **26–27,** 32–33, 36, 40–49, **42–44, 46–47**

intertidal zone, 1–2, 3
Irish moss, **4–5, 14–15**

jellyfish, **42–44**

killifish, **4–5, 22–23**

limpets, 8, 20–28
lobsters, **46–47**

mollusks, **26–27**
    See also clams, oysters, mussels,
        scallops, snails
movement
    of anemones and jellyfish, **42–
        43,** 48
    of blennies and killifish, **22–23**
    of crabs, lobsters, and shrimp,
        46–47
    of scallops, **26,** 45
    of sea urchins, 40
    of snails, 31–32
mud snails, 31
mussels, 8, 18, **26–27,** 28, 33, 36,
    40–45

oceans, 1, **2,** 52–54, **53**
oysters, **26–27,** 33, 36

periwinkles, **4–5,** 7, **26–27**
photosynthesis, 9, **12,** 39, 52
phytoplankton, **41,** 52
plankton, **4–5,** 37, 39–40, **41**
    as food, 40, **42–44,** 45, 48
    See also phytoplankton,
        zooplankton
pollution, 49, 51–54
polyp, **42–44**
Portuguese man-of-war, **42–44**
prawns, **46–47**

rockweeds, **4–5,** 13, **14–15,** 33,
    52

sand dollars, **4–5, 34–35**
scallops, **4–5, 26–27,** 45
scavenging, **26–27,** 31, **46–47**
sculpins, **4–5, 22–23**
sea lettuce, **4–5, 14–15,** 52
sea stars, **4–5,** 8, 16, **34–35**
    hunting by, 32–33
sea urchins, **4–5,** 8, 16, **34–35,**
    40
seaweeds
    See algae
sea worms, 16, 29, 49
shells, 18–20, **26–27,** 28, 29, 48
    hermit crabs and, **24–25,** 29
shrimp, **4–5,** 16, **46–47,** 49
snails, **4–5,** 16, 18, **26–27,** 29
    as food, 33
    babies of, 20, 49
    grazing by, 33–36
    hunting by, 36
    movement by, 31–32
    scavenging by, 31
    See also limpets, mud snails,
        periwinkles, whelks

tides, 1, 2, **2**

water bugs, 16, 29
whelks, **26–27**
winged kelp, **14–15**

zooplankton, **41**